NOTES FOR COMPANY DRIVERS

PETER CHILD

Benbow Publications

© Copyright 2005 by Peter Child

Peter Child has asserted his right under the Copyright, Designs and Patents Act, 1988 to be identified as the author of this work.

All rights reserved. No part of this publication may be reproduced, stored in a retrieval system, or transmitted in any form or by any means, electronic, mechanical photocopying, recording or otherwise without the prior permission of the copyright owner.

Published in 2005 by Benbow Publications

British Library
Cataloguing in Publication Data.

ISBN : 0 9540910 4 3

Printed by Lightning Source UK Limited,
6 Precedent Drive, Rooksley,
Milton Keynes, MK13 8PR

First Edition

OTHER TITLES BY THE AUTHOR

VEHICLE PAINTER'S NOTES

VEHICLE FINE FINISHING

VEHICLE FABRICATIONS IN G.R.P.

NOTES FOR GOOD DRIVERS

FICTION

MARSEILLE TAXI

AUGUST IN GRAMBOIS

CHRISTMAS IN MARSEILLE

INTRODUCTION

With new proposed legislation aimed at both business and company drivers it is important that every effort must be made to reduce the number of road accidents that involve drivers on business.

The Government plans are both far reaching and quite draconian with management facing heavy fines or imprisonment if they have been found to be negligent in the training, management and care of employees who drive on business.

Drivers also have a duty of care and responsibility and must realise that they are part of the company team which must dedicate itself to the safety of each individual as well as the well being of the company.

The statistics and opinions in this book will hopefully draw every driver's attention to the fact that driving today on Britain's overcrowded and congested roads can be a dangerous and hazardous adventure, no matter how experienced the driver may be.

A relaxed and 'can't happen to me' approach must be consigned to the past as business drivers now face the reality of the proposed laws and ever increasing traffic volumes.

It is important that a 'safety style' of driving be developed by all drivers. It is a simple matter of attitude and thinking positively about the important business of driving from point A to point B without incident. The comments and advice contained in this book will hopefully change a driver's perception of motoring and enable them to re-examine their approach to an every day activity, as well as making companies aware of the new responsibilities placed upon them.

Peter Child

AUTHOR'S DRIVING CV

- Passed driving test in May 1958

- Driving Instructor in 1962 for the Wessex School of Motoring in Ilford, Essex..

- Passed Advanced Driving Test in March 1963 and became a member of the Institute of Advanced Motorists.

- Became a Technical Representative for the Automotive Refinishing Division of a Major Paint Conglomorate. Drove throughout the UK on business for over fifteen years with an average of 50,000 miles per year.

- Designed, built and tested specialist sports cars for four years.

- Joined Aston Martin Lagonda Ltd by invitation as Quality Manager and Chief Road Test Driver. Test drove every Aston Martin and Lagonda built from 1983 to 1991. This included high speed testing of all models including the Zagato Coupes and testing in the USA from the Aston Martin workshops in Connecticut.

- Instructed by Aston Martin Lagonda Ltd in 1991 to evaluate the 'Drive and Survive' course at Ford Motorsport, Boreham circuit, for future training of Aston Martin test drivers.

- Became a consultant to the motor industry driving an average of 30,000 miles a year before retiring.

- Driven over 3 million miles in the UK, Europe and the USA without accident.

****

The author has been a pilot since 1970 and holds a multi engine rating, his air safety training has been the basis for the development of his 'safety style' of driving.

CONTENTS

NOTE	PAGE
Proposed legislation	1
Company action	3
Effects on the employee	9
Fit to drive	13
Smooth driving	16
Road conditions	17
Weather conditions	19
Weather trapped	23
Night driving	26
Motorway driving	28
Road rage – how to cope	30
Congestion – how to cope	32
Accidents – how to cope	34
Mobile telephones	38
The Police	38
Conclusions	40

PROPOSED LEGISLATION

The Government will present a timetable for corporate liability legislation which was originally outlined in the Labour party's 1997 manifesto. The legislation is designed to bring companies, who at present, are not managing occupational driving risks within health and safety management systems, into line.

Under the 1974 Health and Safety at Work Act and the 1999 management of Health and Safety at Work Regulations, prosecutions can be brought forward but the corporate manslaughter legislation will become more focused making the responsibilities of the employer more explicit.

It is expected that if criminal or civil proceedings follow an accident involving a person driving on business, the courts will use the new Health and Safety Executive guidelines as a marker for assessing whether or not a company had a comprehensive risk management strategy.

Companies that fail to act on these guidelines run the risk of large fines and Directors and senior managers will also face fines or imprisonment.

Police investigations after an accident will focus in on demands placed on the driver by management as well as vehicle maintenance and reason for the journey. They will investigate if management 'failures' contributed to the accident. If 'failures' are revealed then the HSE may also take action against the company, it's Directors and management, in addition to the Police prosecution of the driver.

The HSE guidelines focus on the following:

> Driver training
> Driver competency
> Health and fitness of the driver
> Vehicle suitability
> Vehicle condition
> Safety equipment fitted to the vehicle
> Driver access to safety information
> Vehicle ergonomics
> Route planning
> Travel time and distance
> Poor weather risks

Professionally designed risk assessment based on vehicle and employee audits will be required.

If an employee uses their own vehicle on company business the employer is still fully responsible under the legislation. This can have serious consequences for the company as it has no control over the type of vehicle or its condition being used by the employee. The question of proper insurance cover is also raised.

A recent survey of 400 fleets showed that 70% were not protecting themselves from the costs of prosecution following a work related traffic accident. Also highlighted were the facts that almost 30% of companies had no procedures for checking privately owned car insurance and over 60% of companies did not limit the working hours that employees drive on business.

The survey also showed that almost 60% of employers

did not check driving licences when employing staff. Of the 40% who did check at the recruiting stage only 12% carried out any regular checks thereafter.

Government figures show that on average there are 20 fatalities and 250 serious injuries every week involving drivers on business.

The losses to UK business, as a result of road accidents, amount to £2.7 billion each year and the cost to the taxpayer is a further £1 billion.

The Government target is a 40% reduction in the number of people killed and injured by 2010.

The first recorded traffic fatality was in 1898 when Henry Lindfield set off from Brighton to drive to London and died as a result of an accident, since then over 20 million people have been killed world wide.

COMPANY ACTION

It is important that companies take this proposed new legislation very seriously and implement action plans as soon as possible to comply.

Initiate a professionally designed risk assessment profile for all the vehicles in the fleet as well as an employee audit for every person who drives and is likely to drive.

Ensure that all vehicle servicing and maintenance is carried out at the manufacturers designated mileage. Ensure that tyres are checked at very short intervals.

Rapid acceleration, heavy braking and fast cornering can cause rapid tyre wear and expose the driver and the company to danger and prosecution.

Implement a driver assessment and training plan.

DRIVER TRAINING

Commence a driver training and a review of competence programme. There are many excellent advanced driving courses available run by the Institute of Advanced Motorists, the RAC the AA and many other highly qualified organisations. These organisations will report to the company on the competence of every driver who undertakes the course. Companies whose drivers attend such courses can normally negotiate a reduction in insurance premiums.

36% of respondents to a recent survey by the Association of Car Fleet Operators claimed that they did not have an accident problem and therefore did not require driver training. A further 22% claimed the costs of training were prohibitive, 16% were too busy to allocate driver time and 27% had not even considered training.

Check all driving licences at recruitment and annually thereafter with demands in employment contracts that any accident or motoring conviction be notified to the company immediately.

Ensure that driving hours are monitored and that excessive driving time is not allowed. All drivers should stop every two hours for a comfort and rest break. Long distance journeys may mean drivers having to stop overnight. at extra cost to business expenses but necessary to prevent prosecution if tiredness is proved to be a factor in an accident.

Fatigue causes the death of over 300 drivers a year. When a driver falls asleep at the wheel they simply crash headlong into another vehicle or obstacle. Police investigations at the scene show that there are no skid marks or any other sign that the driver was taking avoiding action. This is positive proof that the driver fell asleep and will be presented during any prosecution.

HEALTH AND FITNESS

Ensure the health and fitness of the driver and if there is doubt then the company must insist on a medical examination. Poor or slowly failing eye sight is a particular problem often un noticed that must be checked regularly. The only official eye test is at the point of the driving test when the applicant is requested to read a vehicle number plate at 20.5 metres in daylight. This is most unsatisfactory and the official figures show that 50% of drivers require spectacles to drive safely and almost 60% suffer with poor night vision. Government figures show that 68% of accidents happen during the hours of darkness. Traffic Police now are equipped with roadside eye test equipment and can order a driver to take the test when stopped. There have been reported cases where the Police have refused to allow the driver to continue their journey after failing the test.

VEHICLE SUITABILITY

Ensure that the company vehicles are suitable for the work that they are required to do safely and economically. So much status revolves around the company car and too often status clouds the judgement of management who are tasked with purchasing or leasing the correct and most suitable vehicles. In the event of an accident where the employee is found culpable and prosecution follows then the Health and Safety Executive will take into account the type of vehicle involved and its suitability.

VEHICLE CONDITION

The vehicle condition must be maintained to full manufacturer's specification regardless of cost and any lapses in servicing times and mileages will be investigated after an accident and Directors and senior management will be held accountable to the court for such lapses.

SAFETY EQUIPMENT

Safety equipment such as seat belts, air bags, fire extinguishers and first aid kits must be fitted and in full working order at all times. Any shortfall with equipment will be followed up and presented during prosecution.

DRIVER ACCESS TO SAFETY INFORMATION

It is necessary for all company drivers to be fully trained in the use of all safety equipment carried on board the vehicle and also it must be demonstrated by the company that every driver has quick and direct access to all the information regarding the use of the equipment in an emergency.

VEHICLE ERGONOMICS

Vehicle choice and its ergonomics will also be taken into account by the Health and Safety Executive in the event of prosecution. As an example, it would be advisable to have vehicles with power assisted steering fitted to lessen the steering load and reduce fatigue levels. Many other areas must be brought into focus, such as the access to the boot, does it have a too high threshold causing a driver to lift samples etc un necessarily high to load and unload? The driver's safe distance position in relation to the steering wheel in the event of air bag deployment is another important consideration. Careful examination of the work that the vehicle and driver are expected to complete in the day to day business activity must be carried out by the management in charge of vehicle procurement, ensuring that the vehicle and its ergonomics are suitable.

ROUTE PLANNING

Under the proposed new legislation route planning and its effect on the employee's exposure to hazards and fatigue will be examined in the event of an accident where the employee faces Police prosecution. Route planning is an important part of the company's business activity which ensures the best use of employee's valuable time, keeping mileage and fuel costs at the lowest possible level whilst giving the best service to clients and customers.

TRAVEL TIME AND DISTANCE

In the event of an accident involving an employee, travel time and distance will be investigated by the Police as part of the prosecution. Company records will clearly show how far a driver has travelled in a time period, which will the give the average speed as well as highlighting any comfort and rest breaks taken or missed, during the journey, up to the point of accident.

WEATHER RISKS

Bad weather warnings from the Met Office regarding hazardous driving conditions must be carefully noted, particularly in the area where employees might be driving on company business. If the management responsible for the day to day driving activity ignores such warnings and there is a weather related accident, the company will face a full investigation prior to prosecution.

COMPANY ACTION

It must now be realised and accepted by the senior management of a company that compliance to this proposed legislation, where the Health and Safety Executive regards the employee driving on business as an extension to the office or workplace, is essential to avoid personal as well as company prosecution.

Only by planning to meet every aspect of the legislation will Directors, senior management and the company be safe from fines or imprisonment in the event of an accident where Police prosecution follows. It is a serious situation that requires a serious response.

EFFECTS ON THE EMPLOYEE

In the light of the proposed legislation, the employee who travels on company business must review entirely his or her attitude to vehicle and road use. A thoughtful and 'safety style' of driving must be developed and work in harmony with the companies plans to ensure that accident free journeys on business are the norm. This is the same attitude practised by pilots as they fly millions of passengers, millions of miles to destinations all over the world in great safety.

Pilots, Air Traffic Controllers and Aircraft Maintenance Engineers are all part of a team operating to keep aircraft and passengers in absolute safety. This collective and professional approach to commercial air operations has made flying the safest form of travel. All drivers can learn from it.

Pilots undergo safety drills and medical examinations every six months and from the very start of pilot training, the safe conduct of each flight is always the highest priority.

Company drivers can develop the same approach to a 'safety style' of driving by examining their attitude to each journey they undertake no matter how experienced they may be.

The driver is like the pilot, part of a team, with the company management controlling journeys and times, whilst the maintenance engineer is the local main agent for the vehicle.

The Civil Aviation Authority produce a little safety aid note for General Aviation pilots to keep their minds fully focused on their fitness to fly and it works for drivers as well. It is: **I'M SAFE**.

I : Illness.
Coughs, colds and minor ailments will reduce your sensory abilities and reduce concentration. More serious complaints can make you a dangerous liability to yourself and other road users.

M : Medication
Any medication can have an effect on your ability to drive safely. Side effects such as drowsiness can seriously impair your driving and you must resist the temptation to venture out unless your Doctor gives you absolute clearance to drive.

S : Stress

Stress levels affect people in different ways, but it is true to say that stress has an adverse effect on a driver's ability to concentrate. It is a distraction if a driver is concerned or feels pressured in some way and distraction is a major cause of accidents.

A : Alcohol

Any alcohol consumption will slow a driver's reactive times. To show the effects of alcohol the RAF set up comparison tests between two fighter pilots. Both pilots were very fit with lightning fast reactions. One was given a pint of beer to drink and then the tests were repeated. The pilot who had one drink was measurably slower on test, so surely a middle aged person, perhaps slightly overweight, would be much slower reacting to any road situation.   DO NOT DRINK AND DRIVE.

F : Fatigue

Tiredness is an insidious killer. I creeps up on a driver by stealth. You must watch for the signs and once aware of the situation you must stop as soon as it safe to do so. Either go for a walk and then have a coffee or, if you realise you are too tired to continue, lock yourself in the car and go to sleep.

E : Eating

It is dangerous to eat whilst driving as it is another distraction. If the police observe you eating or drinking whilst in control of a vehicle, and that includes standing still in a jam or at traffic lights, they have the power to prosecute you for driving without due care and attention.

It is important for a driver to do everything possible to lessen the risk of an accident. Being fit and ready to drive, coupled with the right attitude and ensuring that your car is serviced and in good order, is the start to a safe day behind the wheel.

Every driver owes it to their family, friends and the company to ensure they return safely home after work. Tragically, the official figures show that there are 20 fatalities and 250 injuries every week involving drivers on business.

To avoid becoming another statistic, start re evaluating your driving ability and approach to the business of getting safely from point A to point B. Everyone knows when their driving standard has slipped. If a driver cuts in too soon after overtaking another vehicle, drives too close to the car in front, changes lanes on a motorway without looking, all causes of motorway accidents that lead to death, injury and at the very least, badly damaged vehicles. Not to mention the long queues of stationary traffic that build up behind the accident polluting the atmosphere with their exhaust fumes.

It is easy to drive in a considerate and relaxed manner. Give plenty of space between you and the car that you have overtaken. Keep well back from the car in front on a motorway, and if another driver overtakes you on the inside and jumps in front, then drop back further.

Change lanes with care and remember that the danger on motorways usually comes from behind. Whether you are driving on motorways or through congested towns and city centres, the same rules of 'safety style' and good driving apply and they are patience and consideration. Practise this approach every day and you will find that you suffer less stress and your journey times are just as short as they were before.

Some company drivers do admit to dangerous habits as the Lex survey 'Driving for Safer Company Motoring' showed. Although they are in a minority it does indicate driver's attitudes to company owned vehicles. The survey found that 80% of drivers exceeded the motorway speed limit and were more likely to overtake on the inside. 40% of business drivers admitted to tailgating whilst only 18% of private motorists admitted to this dangerous practice.

Be prepared that the new proposed legislation will force your company to take more control of your day to day business driving activity. Route planning, driving times, mileages as well as driver training will become part of the norm. Accept this change openly and welcome it, and remember that it is being driven by Government legislation with very serious consequences for Directors, management and the company. You as an employee, driving safely on business, are key and critical to the success of the operation. You are the pilot and you are in command.

FIT TO DRIVE

When you apply to take your driving test you declare that you are fit to drive and the examiner requires you to read a car number plate 20.5 metres away. This is done in daylight and there is doubt whether the statutory 20.5

metres is measured accurately. This is the only medical examination that a driver is required to take and the examination is carried out by a person who is not a qualified optician. This means that by default, it is up to the individual person to assess their medical condition throughout their life until they reach the age of seventy.

At the very least have your sight checked by a qualified optician regularly, it could save your life as well as someone else's. Poor and deteriorating vision is of concern as it generally happens slowly with age. Official figures show that over 50% of drivers need to wear spectacles and as 68% of accidents happen during the hours of darkness, poor night vision is certainly a factor that must be considered.

You must be fit and well to drive on today's busy road network. Being alert, concentration and awareness are essential for safe driving and these all fall to lower standards if you are unwell. Do not fall into the trap of 'pressing on regardless' because it can lead to a disastrous accident with very serious consequences. Every driver needs all their faculties to cope safely and as the day proceeds and tiredness comes into the equation then any illness will rapidly take more of a hold on the driver's ability.

Tiredness is a killer and it is now proven that many late night and early morning accidents are caused by drivers falling asleep behind the wheel. The Police know, by the absence of skid marks, that the dead or injured driver was asleep as the collision occurred. Ploughing into a motorway bridge or a large commercial vehicle will obviously result in the most serious accident.

So, when you feel tired, stop for a break, have a walk and a coffee and reconsider how you feel. If you are still feeling tired, then you must lock yourself in the car and sleep. It is a good idea to keep a blanket in the boot for just such an emergency. You should stop every two hours for a comfort break and a drink. Many business drivers will press on because it is vital that they call on the customer on time, but a planned journey should incorporate these short recovery breaks and if the alternative is a road accident which prevents the customer call, then the best course of action is to take the comfort break.

Alcohol and drugs must be avoided at all costs and the risks associated with driving while under the influence are almost too serious to contemplate. First, there is the possibility that the drunk or drugged driver may kill or injure some other totally innocent road users. Then there is the Police prosecution which will lead to a fine or imprisonment as well as a driving ban, which in the case of drivers whose job requires them to use a car for business, which could lead to dismissal from the company. It is imperative that after a good night out, either a taxi ride home or being driven by a non drinking family member, is the answer. Check that you are still not over the limit the next morning.

A recent Lex survey discovered that 4% of company drivers had driven over the legal alcohol limit in the previous twelve months. It also revealed a disturbing level of irresponsibility by drivers with less than 60% agreeing that it was dangerous.

To be fit to drive safely rests entirely with the person concerned. The driver must feel well, be free of alcohol or drugs and be ready to focus their full concentration to the driving ahead. If you are not fit then do not drive, instead contact the boss and inform him, mindful of the new legislation he will be glad you made the right decision.

SMOOTH DRIVING

Smooth driving at any speed contributes to safety, less fuel consumption and most important, less fatigue for the driver and passengers.

Driving smoothly will ensure that the vehicle remains under good control and it is particularly important when driving in slippery or icy conditions. Smooth acceleration, steering or braking will minimise any sliding or skidding. Erratic handling in dry conditions will cause excessive tyre, steering and brake wear as well as giving a tiring ride. High wear rates on all moving parts automatically increases the cost of maintenance and reduces the financial effectiveness of the company vehicle.

Smooth input to the vehicle control becomes more important and critical to vehicle safety as the speed increases. At high speed it becomes necessary to have very little input into the steering for the car to move quite dramatically and it essential that that input is smooth.
As the world is being urged to be 'greener' and slow down the 'greenhouse effect' the use of fossil fuels

comes into focus. If all drivers accelerated smoothly every time they moved off then the less fuel burnt would make a contribution to cleaner and a less polluted atmosphere. Heavy and sustained acceleration practice in any vehicle, no matter how economic, will increase fuel consumption dramatically.

Smooth braking will give better vehicle control early on in the manoeuvre and bring down the speed progressively as the momentum reduces. If the driver is braking to a full stop, approaching traffic lights for instance, early smooth braking will ensure that the vehicle will stop without being a hazard to following traffic, also the driver and any passengers will not be uncomfortably pushed forward. Emergency braking is now assisted by ABS systems which have increased vehicle control under heavy and sustained braking and made a real contribution to road safety.

Steering smoothly through corners and bends will ensure the vehicle response is smooth and balanced and the momentum that develops allows good times to be achieved on journey routes.

Smooth driving reduces fuel consumption, wear and tear on the vehicle and most important of all, it ensures that driver fatigue is minimised.

ROAD CONDITIONS

Road conditions play a major part in vehicle control and therefore safety. During every journey a driver will experience many different types of road surface and condition which play a part in how well the vehicle remains in safe control.

The only contact with the road surface are the four tyre imprints. On average these are about the same area as the sole of a man's shoe. The vehicle is therefore driving, steering and braking through a very small surface area that is in contact with the road at any one moment.

Poor road surface or wet and slippery conditions mean that the tyres will have less adhesion to the surface than when the road is dry. This fact must be taken into account and although tyre technology continues to advance the road adhesion that they give the vehicle can be readily upset by erratic driver input to the vehicle control. From high speed and sustained driving on motorways to narrow roads with potholes the tyres have to cope in all weathers and with all conditions. It is imperative that tyres are regularly checked for damage, pressure and tread depth.

Some older concrete road surfaces are ridged and will cause 'rumble' as well as tyre vibration. This can happen at various speed ranges and can be off putting to the unwary driver.

Smooth tarmac surfaces appear to become greasy and very slippery after a light rain shower. This is due to a film of oil, fuel, un burnt diesel and rubber contaminates lying on the surface. This is a situation where tyres have to work hard to obtain and hold the grip required for safe driving.

Braking distances will vary depending on whether the road is wet or dry as well as its actual surface material.

Many minor roads are often pot holed and some surfaces may be broken away at the edges. This is cause for concern because damage may occur to the inside wall of tyres which can not be readily seen when carrying out visual checks. If a driver suspects that damage has occurred after negotiating poor roads then the vehicle should be taken to a tyre fitting company as soon as possible for investigation. Sudden tyre deflation as a result of damage, at high speed on a motorway can be very hazardous.

Road camber can vary and although warning signs regarding adverse camber are normally present all drivers should be aware of this road condition, which can be very unsettling, especially in wet conditions.

In very heavy rain the problem of standing water on road surfaces is a challenge to the tyre tread. Its ability to move the water and give surface contact to the road surface is helped by the vehicle being driven at a lower speed. It is imperative for a driver to reduce speed considerably to maintain safe vehicle control and avoid aquaplaning.

WEATHER CONDITIONS

Every aspect of the weather has some effect on a vehicle and its occupants. The heart of the matter is whether a driver is able to understand what these effects are having on the safety margins of the journey. Under the new legislation, management responsible for day to day business driving activity will be held responsible if, after weather warnings, an employee is involved in a weather related accident.

It is the top requirement when driving to be fully aware of the weather and its impact on the vehicle. For instance, if there is a sudden down pour of rain combined with squally winds it would be foolhardy to drive at 70 mph on an exposed motorway. Speed must be reduced to maintain safe, clear vision ahead through road spray as well as being able to cope with side buffeting from the wind. The driver's awareness of the conditions should temper their judgement as to how fast they drive and how early they can anticipate hazards that may occur.

The Effects of Rain

Depending how hard it is raining the hazard will vary. For instance, lashing rain accompanied by high wind should mean a considerable reduction in the driver's planned speed. Visibility will be badly affected, tyre contact on the road surface will be lessened and aqua planning can take place if tyres are worn and the tread depth is low. Skidding or sliding may result in the event of a sudden braking or steering manoeuvre.

Light rain after a dry spell will always leave the road surface greasy and slippery. These two extremes will always hold hazards for the unwary and combined with poor visibility, particularly at night, they can cause dangerous situations. It is a requirement of the law to drive with dipped headlights in the rain.

The Effects of Snow

It is essential that if a driver has to drive in snow conditions they must be prepared mentally and physically. The driver's attitude to the driving and the problems that may occur will ensure that the necessary journey is completed safely. Physically the driver must remain alert and ensure that a shovel, blankets, food, hot drinks and a mobile telephone are carried in the vehicle.

Depending on the rate of snow fall, it will affect decisions on road speed and planned distance. If the snow is turning to slush as it hits the surface then this will allow a slightly higher speed than if the snow is lying on the road and compacted down. Normally the gritters have been out when snow is forecast but sometimes with temperature change and the suddenness the driver may encounter un treated roads. At night in snow conditions, drivers can be mesmerised by the snowflakes coming towards them in the headlight beams. A driver may become tired quickly and must be aware of fatigue. It is better stop and rest rather than push on in the hope that the conditions will improve. In the event of a breakdown or if the vehicle becomes stuck, then the driver should remain in the vehicle and call for assistance.

The Effects of Fog

Visibility is the obvious hazard and the situation becomes more dangerous when the fog is patchy. A driver can be in relatively light misty conditions and then suddenly engulfed in thick fog, this is when collisions occur. The driver in front has hit the dense fog and starts braking heavily and as the brake lights come into view the following driver has to brake harder to make up for reaction time. Eventually, unless all the vehicles are well spaced back and anticipating the conditions, then collisions take place. It is a question of being seen as well as seeing and it is essential that rear fog lights are illuminated in these dangerous conditions. Do not attempt to drive in fog unless the planned journey is absolutely necessary.

Effects of the Sun

There are two major effects of the sun that cause a hazard to the driver. First, when the sun is low on the horizon and the motorist is driving into it. Unless wearing suitable sun glasses and having the sun visors in the best position, the driver's vision is impaired to a degree, depending on the brightness of the sun. Secondly, when the sun is behind the vehicle the reflection of bright work of vehicles in front and those travelling in the opposite direction can 'flash blind' a driver momentarily. This can be dangerous as a driver's vision can be impaired and constant flashing into the eyes is not to be recommended. Suitable sunglasses are the answer, but if the brightness is still too much to cope with, then stop somewhere safely and take a break.

Either the sun will set or rise further making it safe to proceed. Be aware that when the sun is low and shining into the vehicle from either side depending on the vehicle's direction, the trees along the roadside can cause a flickering effect within the vehicle. This can be disorientating as well as distracting. Move sun visors to the side as soon as possible.

WEATHER TRAPPED

The weather in Great Britain plays a significant part in the lives of the population. Other countries seem to have a climate but we experience 'weather'.

It effects everything from sporting fixtures to garden fetes and barbeques. The weather can be good as well as bad and unpredictable. It makes a large contribution to the dangers and hazards of driving. When difficult conditions exist drivers must try to minimise their effects on safety.

Check the weather forecast before setting out on any journey.

During the winter months be prepared for just about every eventuality.

Sometimes the weather forecast mentions everything imaginable and it is surprising the variance in conditions throughout this small island.

Before setting off check the vehicle for lights, indicators, windscreen wipers and washers. Check oil and all fluid levels plus the spare tyre. Take a blanket, food, chocolate, a hot drink in a thermos flask and a shovel. Ensure that there is ample fuel on board for the planned journey plus a reserve amount. Be prepared and expect everything the weather forecast promised.

Rain followed by flooding is becoming the norm and it is a fact that a third of all accidents occur in the rain. This shows that the combination of poor visibility and less grip and control on the road surface which contributes to the hazard of driving. A driver can lessen the risk of these effects by keeping extra an safe distance between vehicles and ensuring that the wipers and demister are working efficiently. In poor visibility dipped headlights must be used to ensure all road users are clearly visible.

When approaching a flooded section of road a driver must decide whether to drive through or turn round and follow a different route. If the decision is to proceed the following advice will be helpful:

Slow the vehicle down to walking pace and engage first gear as the flooded area is reached.

Proceed slowly to ensure that water splash does not interfere with the electrical system

Keep the engine running fast and slip the clutch, this will ensure that if the water is higher than the exhaust pipe the engine pressure will blow the water away so allowing the engine to keep running.

If the engine does stop, engage first or reverse gear,

then, slip the clutch whilst turn the ignition key and hold it. The engine will crank over and the vehicle can be slowly driven out of the flood by the starter motor. Then the vehicle will dry out and will start and run properly. The use of the starter motor will only work on manual cars. Automatic transmissions will not respond in the same way.

Once out of the flood drive slowly and test the brakes and dry them out before proceeding back to normal speed.

If the vehicle has been through deep water it is advisable to have it fully checked by a garage.

Driving in snow should be avoided unless absolutely necessary, however, sometimes the weather can deteriorate very rapidly so there is no alternative but to proceed. Listen out on the radio for up to date travel information and if the situation is becoming more serious then stop at motorway service area or wayside filling station. It is safer to spend the night there rather than stuck in deep snow and sleeping in the vehicle.

If a driver continues and becomes engulfed in heavy snow then the advice is always to stay with the vehicle. The driver should ensure the car exhaust is clear of snow so that occasionally the engine can be run safely to keep warm. Wrap up in a blanket and settle down until the emergency services arrive.

NIGHT DRIVING

At night everything changes. A pilot with a full licence and many hours experience in daylight may not fly at night until a full programme of training at night is complete and a competence examination passed. It is regarding as that important for pilots and should be regarded the same way by drivers.

Official figures show that 68% of road accidents happen at night, so it is important that drivers are aware of the extra hazards that nightfall brings and prepare to lessen the risks.

First priority is to ensure that the driver's night vision is up to standard, so they must not hesitate to visit an optician for examination. Many people suffer with some degree of night vision defect and a quick check can settle the matter.

Before a night journey the driver should check the vehicle to ensure all lights are working and the headlights are clean.

At night, road speed is very deceptive, and after travelling some distance on a motorway or dual carriageway the driver will believe that the speed is within reason, but a glance at the speedometer will often be a surprise. Speed as a result of momentum builds and as the change is subtle, the driver may not be aware of what is happening. It therefore comes as a surprise when driving off the motorway on the slip road or approaching a roundabout at the end of a dual carriageway, very heavy braking is required to slow the vehicle to a safe speed. The driver should constantly monitor the speedometer at night.

Night driving calls for better judgement of speed and distance. There are now warning signs and rumble strips on the road surface at the end of dual carriageways to advise a driver that there is a roundabout ahead or the road narrows. At night it is much harder to judge the braking distance and for that reason many drivers end up in the middle of a roundabout because they were travelling too fast, even for the modern braking system to cope.

On single carriageways the danger is when a driver or an oncoming motorist attempts to overtake a slower vehicle. It is extremely difficult to judge closing speeds at night with only oncoming headlights to gauge the speed. Overtaking is a hazardous occupation and the best advice is to wait until no other vehicle is coming in the opposite direction before overtaking. It is important to remain patient.

Pedestrians and cyclists can be a real hazard at night, especially in town or city centres when clubs and pubs turn out. People will stagger out and cyclists may wobble unexpectedly so a driver must be prepared for such eventualities. Give everybody and everything a wide berth at night.

When driving at night it is important to be aware of the hazards and if a driver is prepared then it can be pleasant driving with usually less traffic to contend with.

MOTORWAY DRIVING

The fact that immediately after passing a driving test a driver is at liberty to head for the nearest motorway and proceed at a speed of 70 mph, which until then, their driving experience has been usually at 30 mph, appears foolhardy and a loophole in the driving test which requires closing at the earliest opportunity.

No driver on today's motorway network has been formally tested by an examiner and been required to demonstrate their competence to drive on such a highway. This is where advanced driving courses can be invaluable. Under the expert tuition available, driver's may learn to drive on motorways with maximum safety to themselves and other road users, as well as building confidence whilst developing a safety assured driving style.

The motorway should be the safest road to drive on, with all vehicles travelling in the same direction, with a safety crash barrier separating traffic travelling in the opposite direction, and no traffic lights or cross roads to present hazards to the unwary. Unfortunately there are many motorway accidents and they are mainly due to the following:

- Driving too close to the vehicle in front.
- Changing lanes too quickly and failing to look to the side as well as the rear of the vehicle.
- Failing to indicate properly and giving adequate time.
- Falling asleep behind the wheel.

It is not difficult to drive safely on a motorway. All a driver needs to do is to keep a safe distance from the vehicle in front, change lanes slowly after checking the side and rear of the vehicle before manoeuvring whilst indicating properly and taking a comfort and rest break every two hours. It is a mystery to the Traffic Police, who are kept busy attending to the aftermath of many accidents, why drivers will not follow these safe procedures and drive in this simple 'safety style'.

Congested motorways are a fact of modern life and must be recognised as such. Even if the traffic is only moving at 60 mph, that's a mile a minute, as long as there are no accident delays, then every driver will reach their destination in due course.

When joining a motorway down the slip road a driver must accelerate and match the speed of the traffic in the slow lane. The idea is to merge safely into the traffic flow and if it means using up all the distance on the acceleration lane, then that is quite in order.

The driver must keep their lane discipline and when moving from one lane to another for the purposes of overtaking, they should return to the original lane. It has been observed that drivers will often remain in the overtaking, or third lane, indefinitely, whilst the middle and first lane can be carrying relatively light traffic. The Road Research Laboratory has stated that 'if all drivers moved back into the appropriate lanes, it would give a further 40% road space on motorways'. Space well worth having on busy motorways.

If a driver has any form of mechanical failure then they

should move to the hard shoulder as quickly and safely as possible. Summon assistance with a mobile telephone or leave the vehicle with hazard lights on and walk to the nearest emergency telephone. It is advisable not to remain in the vehicle but move to a safe position on an embankment as there have been many accidents caused by motorway traffic colliding with broken down vehicles.

Modern vehicles and the motorway system has unlocked time and distance for all drivers and it is the safest highway to drive on, provided that the simple safety rules are followed.

ROAD RAGE

This unpleasant phenomenon has now appeared and seems to becoming more widespread. Stress and impatience are the prime causes and as roads become more and more congested, the reported incidents of road rage will increase.

A recent survey showed that 3 out of 4 drivers had suffered road rage attack and this seems to be caused by an inability by some to deal with strangers. Almost all drivers believe they are more competent than other road users and wonder why so many other drivers make such bad mistakes.

Travelling has become more difficult because of the lack of planned investment in the road and rail systems for many years. Congestion and delays will be ongoing for some time to come before the necessary improvements are fully in place. It is important for both management and employees to accept this fact and relax into a sensible and realistic frame of mind. Good planning will ensure that achievable call rates can be met safely. If a more sanguine approach is not adopted, then road rage incidents will increase and escalate making the driving experience even more of a nightmare.

Drivers are becoming angry at everything and everyone as their road space is being compressed down by too many strangers. They then reach a point where, if they observe some minor foolish act by another driver, it can trigger an offensive outburst.

Bad experiences at work or at home can set off a final spiral of irritation that ends with a driver behaving badly towards another road user. It is important to try and take the pressure out of every situation and unrealistic expectations of career prospects or personal involvements can manifest themselves in anger and aggression.

Courtesy is the hallmark of good driving and part of the 'safety style' approach. Although, in many instances, courtesy appears to be some what neglected in the modern pace of life, most drivers are reasonable and well behaved.

The way of dealing with road rage is to try to defuse the situation. For example, if an overtaking driver has moved too close to the vehicle being overtaken it may well spark some form of retaliation, such as light flashing or sounding the horn, then if the driver who has caused offence can give a wave and say 'sorry' it will calm the situation. The aggrieved driver may regard the offending driver as a hopeless case, but recognition of the fault will ease the situation and the aggrieved driver will feel content and slightly superior.

At all times one should remain calm and keep taking pressure out of the incident. This approach will save unpleasant abuse and upset that can un-nerve a driver and affect their driving standard for the rest of the journey.

If, in the final analysis, a driver is forced to stop by an out raged motorist, they should keep doors and windows closed and locked and wait for the tirade to finish, as it will eventually. The driver should keep calm and be patient and if the verbal abuse turns to physical violence then try to get the registration number before driving off. Report the incident to the Police as soon as possible.

No driver should ever put up with road rage, this is a civilised country, let us try to keep it that way.

CONGESTION

Congestion is a serious problem and set to get worse in the short term. Under investment and the lack of long term planning by successive Governments has brought the traffic speed down considerably on motorways and trunk roads too small and inadequate to cope with the volumes that were predicted.

Management and employees must clearly understand the implications of road congestion. Good and effective route planning will become an even more essential part of the business activity. It must be recognised that some call rates in certain and heavily congested areas will have to be reduced.

Congestion on the motorways in the southeast is particularly heavy, with the M25, M1, M4, M3 and M40 being prime examples of inadequate road space at certain times during the day. An accident on any of these motorways close to the M25 causes traffic gridlock and some of the jams around London Heathrow as a result have been very severe. The M6 around Birmingham is another hot spot, despite the new toll road to the north, and Manchester, Liverpool, Leeds, Newcastle, Glasgow and Edinburgh all suffer congestion daily.

Plan journey times out of rush hour and if that is not possible the driver should remain calm whilst in congested areas. The realisation that getting angry or frustrated will not alter the amount of traffic ahead will reduce stress levels. The driver may plan a diversion route whilst waiting or if that is not possible then listen to the in car entertainment for relaxation as well as traffic news.

Accept that congestion is a fact and will remain so for some time to come. Management and employees must work together and plan the way forward to allow the company business to proceed effectively.

ACCIDENTS

Accidents are preventable, Commercial Aviation has proved that by a dedicated, professional approach to safety, the risks are minimised and as a result, flying is the safest form of travel.

Official figures show that when a person is involved in a road accident and has injuries that require hospital treatment, the cost to the tax payer at present exceeds £100,000, which equates to £1 billion annually. This is the total cost of Police Officers and Paramedics at the scene, hospital medics plus all the support staff as well as after care professionals. Then there is the commercial cost of vehicle recovery and repair, lost business, sick pay to the employee and insurance costs. For those involved in accidents whilst on business, the annual cost to industry is £2.7 billion.

It is a fact that since the first recorded fatality in 1898 over 20 million people have been killed in road accidents world wide. If a Boeing 747 plunged to earth once a month in Britain there would be a total ban on flying and all aircraft would be grounded. However, it is accepted that approximately the same number of people die on the roads each month and it appears to go un noticed. It is an attitude and mind set that must be changed. The new legislation will be an attempt to ensure business drivers and their management review past practices and focus on the safety issues.

The Road Research laboratory and the Traffic Police agree that one third of accidents are speed related and the other two thirds are the result of careless driving.

Recent figures show that where speed cameras have been installed the accident rate has fallen by 50%. For every one mile per hour reduction in speed equates to a 5% drop in accident rate.

It now is time for the careless and poor driving behaviour to come under careful scrutiny.

Drivers should always be prepared for the unexpected. As an example, DEFRA research has shown that in 2003, deer wandering on to roads have caused 42,000 accidents costing £10.5 million in damage to vehicles along with 15 deaths.

The motoring public has been subjected for a considerable time to many television programmes demonstrating various makes of vehicles being driven by presenters on runways at aerodromes, where the babble talk is of 0 to 60 in so many seconds with a top speed of a hundred and something, governed down, of course. The power of television is never to be under estimated and as long as these 'test drivers' carry on screaming up and down and spinning round and round the impressionable section of the motoring public will inevitably try to mimic these 'experts'. It probably is in order to drive like this if business customers are situated on a disused aerodrome, but generally most are not, and so any high speed manoeuvring by professional drivers on busy roads is to be avoided.

Spectating is a favourite pastime whether it be television or an accident by the roadside. When watching television the worst than can happen is the viewer might spill their drink. Slowing to observe a recent accident can and often does lead to a low speed collision with the vehicle in front, whose driver has also slowed. A driver must remain very alert at the scene of any accident to ensure that they focus and concentrate on driving safely past the incident.

Statisticians will insist that drivers covering high mileages on business are 'certain to have an accident.' This not the case, many professional drivers, like pilots, complete a lifetime of business driving or flying, without accident. The author has completed over 3 million miles, driving in the UK, Europe and the USA, as well as thirty four years of flying without incident and many colleagues can more than match that record. It can be done by adopting the 'safety style' of driving.

If a driver is involved in an accident then they must:

- Stop immediately.
- Call for help if any person involved has sustained any injury and give clear details of the incident so that the emergency services can respond quickly.
- If the incident is a minor, a scrape or damaged bumper, then exchange details and ensure the make and registration number of the vehicles involved are carefully noted.
- No driver should admit liability at the scene.
- A driver must remain calm and controlled at all times, even if it is obviously the other road user's fault.

- Inform the Police and the company at the earliest opportunity.

Drivers who have suffered an accident will generally agree that the situation developed very quickly and the impact happened very fast indeed. The normal driver response when faced with an oncoming vehicle on the wrong side of the road is to brake as hard and quickly as possible. Unfortunately there often is not enough time or road space to avoid a collision.

Vehicles colliding at any speed is disastrous, and consider the fact that it is the combined speed at the point of impact which is so damaging. If two vehicles collide head on whilst travelling at 30 mph the combined speed and sustained damage is equal to one colliding with a stationary vehicle at 60 mph.

If a driver has carried out every possible manoeuvre on the road to avoid an accident, then finally they should swerve off the road into a ditch, hedge or any available space to ensure that vehicle collision does not occur. It is surprising how vehicles can run off the road and suffer little serious damage. Minor paint and panel damage is inevitable but that is preferable to the serious consequences of a head on impact.

Develop the 'safety style' of driving whilst keeping in mind that accidents are avoidable.

MOBILE PHONES

The reason that legislation has been brought in to stop drivers using hand held 'phones is because the distraction they cause may lead to an accident. It is dangerous to use a hand held 'phone whilst driving and if the vehicle being driven does not have a 'hands free' system, the driver must find a safe place to stop and turn off the ignition before using the 'phone.

Most professional business drivers have the 'hands free' system installed, but they must be aware that if they are found to be using the 'phone at the point of an accident, the Police may prosecute under the 'driving without due care and attention' legislation.

THE POLICE

The Traffic Police are not the enemy of the law abiding, courteous driver, and they never have been. They are a service which, by public consent, uphold the laws which Parliament has debated and passed as necessary for the safety and common good of all road users.

It is the Government of the day that decides on speed limits, road improvements, and taxation levels, not the Police.

An inconsiderate driver speeding passed a school as the children are leaving, deserves to be caught by a radar trap or speed camera, and blaming the Police is lame excuse by the driver for their anti social behaviour in charge of a lethal weapon. Sadly many children are killed and injured when attending school.

It is important to remember and keep in mind that Traffic Police are normally first on the scene of an accident and have to deal with all manner of unpleasant situations, from dead drivers to badly injured passengers. What would make any person angry would be the certain knowledge that some fool driving a car too fast for the conditions, too carelessly or possibly drunk, had caused the death or serious injury of a perfectly innocent road user.

It is certain that the Government will bring in harsher penalties for those who persistently break the law and cause injury and damage to other road users and their vehicles.

If a driver is stopped by the Police then they should be aware that the first few moments of the conversation can affect the outcome.

The officer is doing his duty, so politeness, bearing in mind that he represents the authority of the law, is helpful from the outset. A driver should listen without protestation or argument to what the officer has to say. A driver can be confident that if they have been stopped it is for a good reason. By all means, a driver may put their point of view and those comments will be noted, but in the final analysis the driver can be sure that they have been observed breaking the law. If the driver disagrees with the officer, then they may always attend the Magistrate's court where they are free to put their case forward.

Many Police forces are using un-marked cars to apprehend drivers who are speeding or driving dangerously, tail gating on a motorway or overtaking on the inside.

If a driver is ordered to stop then they should do so as quickly and safely as possible, listen to the officer, make any point calmly and then go to court if they disagree with any prosecution.

The Police are on our roads to uphold the law and keep all road users in safety.

CONCLUSIONS

It is a fact that new and far reaching legislation will affect they way in which companies and their employees carry on with their daily business activities.

The responsibilities of management will encompass many areas from care, consideration and safety of employees whilst driving on business to realistic work loads and call rates whilst ensuring that all vehicles in the fleet are properly maintained to the vehicle manufacturer's specifications.

The responsibilities of the driver employees is to ensure that they are fit and well and ready to drive in the 'safety style' of driving each working day. They must ensure that they advise their vehicle fleet manager of any incident, accident or mechanical fault that may occur at any time and that includes when the vehicle is used outside working hours on social activity.

Every driver must check their vehicle regularly for fluid levels, tyre and brake wear, wipers and washers, lights and indicators.

Drivers must be ready and open to accept any driver training or assessment that the company deems appropriate and within the scope of a driver training programme. This is not unreasonable and although many drivers feel that after years of driving experience such training or assessment is un-necessary. This is manifestly incorrect as it is a fact that over the years bad habits creep into most driver's performance. In the safe world of Commercial Aviation, all pilots undergo a full safety and aircraft handling check flight every six months with an examiner for as long as they fly. No exceptions are made for any pilot no matter how many hours flown, or years of experience, they all have to have the safety check.

The new proposed legislation is going to have an affect on the way business activity is conducted in this country. To ensure that the legislation is adhered to, companies and their employees must work together as a team. Co-operation and realistic approaches to the day to day problems must become paramount and it is incumbent for both management and employees to work closely together and with complete understanding.

Safety and awareness of other road users needs to go hand in hand and only by setting higher driving standards and then meeting those standards will the accident rate fall. The basic bad driving faults are timeless and go on repeating themselves with the inevitable consequences of more road deaths and injuries. Professional drivers have extra responsibilities and duties of care as they drive high mileages and are exposed for many hours on the road network, and any accident will cause loss to the business.

To continue to drive safely a person must constantly re evaluate their driving style and be self critical of their daily performance. Approach, attitude and evaluation along with patience, courtesy and consideration all play a part in the safe conduct of each and every journey.

The fact that there are 20 fatalities and 250 serious injuries every week involving drivers on business means that unless drivers and company managers address this accident rate the Government legislation will force every one involved, who is deemed culpable, to suffer the consequences of heavy fines or imprisonment.

The inescapable conclusion is that if companies and employees fail to respond then they will have only themselves to blame. Take positive action now and ensure it does not happen to you or your company.